HIDDEN PICTURES

Larry Daste

DOVER PUBLICATIONS, INC.
Mineola, New York

Publisher's Note

In this challenging puzzle book, artist Larry Daste has concealed nearly 300 objects in 24 scenes set in Africa, India, Australia, and the Americas. Picture captions tell you what objects to look for. Feel free to turn the page this way and that to locate rotated objects. When you find them, you can outline them in marker or shade them lightly with a pencil. Try to find all of the hidden objects—which include food, clothing, animals, and maps of the U.S. and some of the states—before you turn to the Solutions, which begin on page 25. If you enjoy coloring, you can color in the pictures as well.

Bibliographical Note

Hidden Pictures is a new work, first published by Dover Publications, Inc., in 2001.

International Standard Book Number: 0-486-41576-7

Manufactured in the United States of America
Dover Publications, Inc., 31 East 2nd Street, Mineola, N.Y. 11501

These West Highland white terriers enjoy frolicking outdoors. But they haven't noticed the 13 objects concealed around them in the yard: an **ice cream scoop**, a **whale**, a **shorthandled hatchet**, a **seahorse**, **2 carrots**, a **socket wrench**, a **crescent shape**, a **garden spade**, a **barbecue fork**, a **hawk**, a **firefighter's ax**, and a **barbecue spoon**.

The hippos didn't spot the 15 objects that don't belong at their favorite watering hole: **4 hearts,** an **olive,** a **bird,** a **snake,** a **radish,** a **pear,** an **ice skate,** a **map of Louisiana,** a **dog biscuit,** a **safety pin,** a **fish,** and a **pencil.**

These elephants haven't noticed the following 11 things during their walk: a **fox's head**, a **squirrel**, a **jet plane**, a **yo-yo**, an **orange slice**, a **banana**, **Robin Hood's cap**, a **boxing glove**, a **fountain pen**, a **parrot**, and a **bowl of popcorn**.

The lion family seems unaware that 12 things are hidden so close to them. Look carefully for: a **backpack,** a **ketchup bottle, pruning shears,** a **peace pipe, bananas,** a **baseball cap, Swiss cheese,** a **toadstool,** a **hand saw,** a **slipper,** a **dinosaur,** and a **crown.**

These sea creatures are too busy to pay attention to 14 things in their tropical paradise: a **baseball bat**, a **key**, a **lifeguard's whistle**, a **shamrock**, a **boomerang**, a **cupcake**, a **bell**, a **caterpillar**, a **cotton swab**, a **rabbit**, a **sweatsock**, a **horseshoe**, a **cane**, and a **woodchuck**.

The sea birds can find the seahorses and octopus, but they can't
locate the following 12 objects: a **pair of eyeglasses**, a **bell**, a
rocket ship, a **paintbrush**, a **pearl ring**, a **bat**, a **wrench**,
an **eel**, a **dinner fork**, a **moth**, a **pigeon**, and a **comb**.

The rhinoceros and crocodile have no idea that the following 17 objects are close at hand: **pliers**, a **bunch of celery stalks**, a **map of California**, **bananas**, a **cowboy boot**, a **flashlight**, a **chair**, an **artichoke**, a **screwdriver**, a **salt shaker**, a **muffin**, a **rabbit's head**, a **metal nut**, a **Civil War cap**, a **bat's head**, a **marching band hat**, and a **caterpillar**.

The charging tiger could find 13 hidden objects if it weren't in such a hurry: a **lollipop**, a **pick ax**, a **tube of toothpaste**, a **crescent moon**, a **balloon on a string**, a **vase**, an **umbrella**, a **drinking straw**, a **bird in flight**, a **fish**, a **coffee mug**, a **toothbrush**, and a **caterpillar**.

The sleeping leopard is too busy dreaming to care about these
17 objects: a **bunch of celery stalks**, a **crescent**, a **party
horn**, **2 thumbtacks**, a **cotton swab**, **2 hearts**, a **hot dog**,
a **carrot**, a **party hat**, a **lobster**, a **wristwatch**, a **hammer**,
a **snow cone and straw**, a **hen**, and a **mushroom**.

Against the background of a slithering snake and tall trees you will discover the following 14 objects: a **handbag**, a **butterfly**, a **railroad spike**, a **strawberry**, a **makeup brush**, a **slingshot**, a **pen nib**, a **hockey stick**, a **tape measure**, a **bolt**, a **pair of lips**, a **spear**, a **parasol**, and an **olive fork**.

These gorillas are surrounded by 12 objects that don't concern them in the least: a **caveman's club,** a **lemon slice,** a **ratchet wrench,** a **comb,** a **map of Florida,** a **piece of birthday cake with candle,** a **mushroom,** a **bald eagle's head,** a **watermelon slice,** a **fish bone,** a **crowbar,** and an **antique musket.**

Eleven objects are concealed among the leaves where
these orangutans are playing: a **pencil**, a **monkey
wrench**, a **woodpecker**, an **apple**, a **bee**, a **quill pen**,
a **pizza slice**, a **book**, a **hair bow**, a **fly**, and a **beetle**.

These cattle are grazing on the plains of our nation's
largest (continental) state. Find the hidden letters that
spell the name of this breed of Texas cattle.

Concealed in this picture of two towering giraffes are 14 objects: a
birthday candle, a **flashlight**, a **peanut**, an **alligator**, a **doughnut**,
a **crescent wrench**, a **dog bone**, a **flute**, a **door key**, a **pig's head**,
a **hairbrush**, a **U.S. map**, a **crab**, and a **mouse**.

Hidden among these kangaroos are the letters that spell the
name of the place where these delightful animals can be found.

Luckily for these chickens, the fox has decided not to make trouble in the henhouse today. Look carefully at the fox and chickens and elsewhere in the picture to locate the 15 concealed objects: a **hatchet,** a **shark,** a **hammer,** a **baseball,** a **feather duster,** a **snow shovel,** a **pineapple,** a **dog's name,** a **putty knife,** an **ice cream bar,** a **shoe,** a **cracked egg,** a **shovel,** a **sailboat,** and a **frog.**

Bears certainly do like honey, as this picture reveals. The picture also contains 13 hidden objects: a **boxing glove**, a **tomahawk**, a **camera**, **2 carrots**, a **kite**, a **Christmas stocking**, a **tortoise**, a **coffee cup**, a **sawfish**, a **butter knife**, a **barbecue fork**, and a **dragon**.

This owl wants to know "who-o-o" has hidden these 12 objects in the picture: a **pair of scissors**, an **eraser**, a **glove**, a **shoe**, a **pair of pliers**, a **trophy**, a **toast slice**, a **fishing rod and reel**, an **apple**, a **marching band hat**, a **thumbtack**, and a **bugle**.

These lions are on the lookout for prey, but they haven't noticed the
11 objects hidden in the picture: an **ice cream bar,** a **clothespin,**
a **snail,** a **teddy bear,** a **puppy,** a **running shoe,** an **ear of corn,**
a **spool of thread,** a **spatula,** a **hairpin,** and a **witch's hat.**

If the elephants took a break from their bath, they might discover the
following 11 objects: a **pony**, a **ruler**, a **diamond ring**, a **work glove**,
a **hand mirror**, an **iron**, a **whisk broom**, an **ice cream cone**,
a **crown**, a **fried egg**, and a **ballpoint pen**.

You would think that these wide-eyed birds would have spotted the 14 things hidden in the picture by now. Find the following items: a **golf club,** an **inchworm,** a **light bulb,** a **dustpan,** a **ladder,** a **baby bottle,** a **flag,** a **musical note,** a **book,** a **thimble,** a **slice of cake,** a **measuring spoon,** a **badminton shuttlecock,** and a **lizard.**

These butterflies are an amazing sight as they flutter about.
Look carefully and you will be able to find the following
14 things hidden among them: a **metal screw**, a **trowel**,
a **matador's hat**, a **needle**, a **dragonfly**, a **soup ladle**,
an **orange slice**, a **mop**, a **drawing pen**, a **slice of cake**,
a **pen knife**, a **crescent moon**, a **maraca**, and a **bottle**.

Watch your step! If these tiny insects were to sting you,
you might react with the words **OUCH! FIRE ANTS!**
Now look carefully at this picture to find the letters
and punctuation for these words.

This diver found more than a shipwreck in the ocean. He also saw the following 23 objects: a **spoon**, a **fork**, a **rat**, a **bowling pin**, a **car key**, a **saucepan**, a **handbag**, an **acorn**, a **turtle**, a **crayon**, a **map of Texas**, a **toothbrush**, a **shoe**, an **ice cream pop**, a **mitten**, a **mallet**, a **dove**, a **hatchet**, a **sewing needle**, an **artist's paintbrush**, a **fried egg**, a **pizza slice**, and a **fishhook**.

Solutions

page 1

page 2

page 3

page 4

page 5

page 6

page 7

page 8

page 9

page 10

page 11

page 12

LONGHORNS
page 13

page 14

AUSTRALIA
page 15

page 16

page 17

page 18

page 19

page 20

page 21

page 22

page 23

page 24